Spirits of My Youth

~ *A Book of Poetry* ~

Carissa Lynn Taylor

PublishAmerica
Baltimore

First printing

PublishAmerica has allowed this work to remain exactly as the author intended, verbatim, without editorial input.

Picture taken by: Cheryl L. Olson.

ISBN: 1-60474-980-6
PUBLISHED BY PUBLISHAMERICA, LLLP
www.publishamerica.com
Baltimore

Printed in the United States of America

This book is dedicated to:

My wonderful Mother, Cheryl Cantara
Lovely Sisters: Lindsey and Anne
And my other Lovely "sisters": Maribeth, Gail, and Hilary

My beautiful children:
My son, Tristan and step-daughter, Cora.

To the rest of my family and friends:
You have touched my life in so many ways.
I love you all, more than words can say!

And, to David…who brought me back to life!

A New Beginning

You made me forget,
Wiped the slate clean.
Your lips on mine
Were all I could feel.

Hands so strong,
So careful, so sweet,
Caressing my skin,
Better than any dream.

Eyes of crystal,
Blue as the sky,
Your body so warm,
Wrapped around me all night.

I can still hear your voice
Whispering in my ear,
I can still fell your breath,
With your cheek brushing my hair.

I had forgotten how to feel,
You showed me the way.
I will carry that with me,
All through my days.

My pain, you took away,
The world again is sane,
Because I spent one night,
In the arms of my best friend.

A Poem for Danny

I want you to know,
I really did care,
And I tried my hardest
To be there
To take you away,
From all the hurt you suffered,
Was what you truly deserved.
To hold you when you needed me,
To take your little hand in mine,
For you there just was not
Nearly enough time.
This poem written from me to you,
Is to say how I feel,
And believe these words are true:
We miss you so much,
It is incredible, my Danny.
I wish I could go back in time,
Just to look at you,
One last time,
And say, "We love you!"

In Loving Memory of:
Danny Rodriquez
1988-1994

25 Things to Know About Women

1. Not all women love to shop. Not all men hate it!

2. Women can drink as well as men, sometimes better.

3. Women tell details—every possible detail imaginable in any event.

4. Women are crude too—yes when we have the house alone, we do the exact same things that men do, we just don't brag about it!

5. We are capable of sleeping with you and being just friends the next day! Get over yourself already. Sex does not mean love.

6. If you are looking for just sex, tell us, we will understand, we don't necessarily like you either!

7. No, we do not always like to cuddle. It's nice before we sleep, but when I am sleeping, get the hell away from me unless you can be quiet, perfectly still, an allow me all the room I need!

8. There is a reason we got to the bathroom in pairs: to discuss you, which would be rude to do directly in front of you at the table.

9. If we look nice in public, that's one thing, but do not expect me to be hanging around the house that way. At home it's sweats all the way!

10. Women hate heels. They are strictly for your benefit.

11. Same with makeup.

12. Same with sexy lingerie!

13. We do like men who can dance. If you take me someplace where there is dancing and you sit in your chair all night, plan on sleeping alone later!

14. That goes for slow dancing. If there is a slow song and a dance floor…Get what I'm saying here?

15. Guess what, there are distinct lanes on the road for a reason, they should not all be used at the same time.

16. If you put a ring on a woman's finger you better be prepared to follow through. Don't just do it because that's the typical next step…that's how homicides happen.

17. If you ask for our opinion, expect an honest answer (for example: yes those shoes are ugly!!!) If you don't ask, we won't offer.

18. Vice versa, we know this. This is why if we don't ask…keep your mouth shut!

19. Do you have hair under that hat? If so, could we see it once in a while?

20. We don't care if you have a guy's night out, as long as it's not every night! Seriously, isn't once a week enough? You guys only sit there and drink and watch TV someplace anyway.

21. Believe it or not, you may still go to a strip club…as long as you bring us with you. We have no problem with this; it might even get you laid later! Just don't keep it a secret.

22. Ditto with porn. This is the 21st century guys, lighten up!

23. The world does not revolve around you, my friends and I have other things to talk about.

24. If you live with or are married to us, this does not mean that you do not still have to be sweet. We still like flowers, dancing and romantic gestures. This is why most domestic partnerships lose out on sex!

25. Most importantly...be truthful, say what you feel. If you love me, tell me, if you don't, tell me that too. If you have something to say, say it now. I'd rather have my feelings hurt now than a broken heart later. Don't be a coward...just speak!

Dark

I feel the tide of the black mist come over me.
I fight to breathe, fight to live, fight to be me.
I have no control as I sink deeper into the dark.
My boundaries and all reason are gone,
Further away I feel myself falling,
As I try to swim back into reality.
The light I can feel as close as the hand of darkness,
That reaches for my soul and mind.
I rise to the surface of my own body again.
I can see, I can hear.
How long will I be allowed to stay,
Before the battle begins again?
In the end it will be a victory, no doubt.
But which side will win?

Able

I did not blame you,
For turning away.
This was not something we had planned.

Though our brief romance,
Needed not persist,
You were supposed to remain my friend.
Instead, you cast me aside.

My rock was gone,
My sure footing fallen away,
The betrayal too grand.

You had my trust,
As well as my heart,
Which you wasted,
With your ignorance.

I should have fled
The moment you entered my life.
If only in our past,
Could we glimpse our future.

Instead, I welcomed your strong arms,
To assist me on my journey,
As I staggered through my misery.

I may be alone.
I am not lonely.
Are you able to speak the same truth?

Walk Away

I felt my poor heart shatter,
Into many pieces tonight,
At the response of my love,
My most precious guiding light.
To take a chance together,
Or to walk away,
That was the question asked.
The answer he could not say.
To not be sure now,
About the way he feels,
A new question I am forced to ask,
"Is his love for real?"
To walk away forever,
And have us never knowing,
Or take a walk together,
Our memories brightly growing.
"Will we last, or will we not?"
Always on the tip of our tongue.
To never give it a try,
Is a battle never won.

All It Takes

All it takes is one wonderful night,
To ruin everything.
All because of one unspoken truth
And the truth you would not hear.
It may not be what you wanted to know,
That did not make it a lie.

I will never regret
Laying in your arms, and holding you tight.
Feeling your kiss and tender touch,
Are moments that are burned
In my memory forever.

Although I love you,
I live without you.
But for one wonderful night,
You took my breath away,
And loved me more
Than anyone ever will again.

All Alone

Into your arms I ran,
Though my mind knew not to go.
I gave my heart to you,
And thought you had done the same.
You were the one who rescued me,
And then turned me out into the cold.
All my trust and love were yours,
You promised to hold me close.
Instead you led me blindly,
Through all your lies and deceit.
I cannot understand
How you can take a fragile heart,
For your own games,
Only to break into pieces,
What little of me had remained.
I will get through this,
I will make myself strong.
Someday I will be happy,
And you will still be alone.

Alluring Blaze

I watch with horror,
And some fascination,
As her magnificent, splendor,
Consumes all in her path.

Blazing, red tendrils,
Glide all around,
As long, disastrous fingers,
Reduces the world to ash.

Alluring and mesmerizing,
Bold in her destruction,
The sirens wail loudly into the night,
Appearing at last,
To tame the hostile beast.

All Is Well?

On a deep dark night,
At twelve o'clock noon,
I stepped out onto my porch,
To see the full moon.
My knight in shining armor,
Surfed up to my door,
To retrieve the umbrella,
He had left here before.
I remember that noon,
So warm, so bright,
And at the same time,
A dark, chilling night.
As he drove away,
I heard him exclaim,
"I love you Honey,
Though I do forget your name."
"All is well, that ends well",
I guess you could say.
But nothing can be quite right,
When your night is also your day.

Being a Mom, Being Me

"But you're a Mom", you exclaim,
Your voice high and shrill,
Like I should be knitting,
Very quiet and still.

It is true things have changed,
So quickly, so much,
But, I have the old me,
Still keeping in touch.

Cleaning the house,
Doesn't qualify as fun,
But I get my joys later,
Playing cars with my son.

I am older now,
And I do have a toddler,
Who decides that it means,
I can't like Harry Potter?

I spend my days,
Raising my son, holding him tight,
Every now and then,
I breakaway,
And sing Kelly with all of my might.

I like the same music,
The same movies and books,
Reading Stephen King,
Has nothing to do with how I cook.

"But, you go to bed early,
Just like an old lady!"
And I wake early too,
And watch Matt with my baby.

Always, Forever

He makes my heart all a flutter
I could never want another.
His crystal eyes, blue as the sea
My soul moves, when he looks at me.
Golden hair that shines like the sun
I know for me, he is the one.
I dream of him every night
In his arms everything feels so right.
He makes me feel so warm and safe
Next to him is my favorite place.
He says "I Love You", with such truth
I will never need for other proof.
He holds me tight when we're together
As I pray we will be, Always, Forever.

Wonderland

It seems like a dream,
It's beauty to behold,
Just like a wonderland,
From the stories of old.

I walk on white velvet,
Spread down the lane,
While archways of glass,
Rise over my head.

From the sky diamonds fall,
Around me everywhere.
I hear their small chiming,
As they land in my hair.

The silence is deafening,
Yet so soft and sweet,
The only sound I hear
Is my own heartbeat.

The strong wind surrounds me,
Waking me from my dream,
And the world has changed back,
From which it just seemed.

No longer a wonderland,
From the stories of old,
Just the same winter,
So long and so cold.

Brightly Shining Star

We thought of you today.
We think of you everyday.
After all this time,
We still cannot believe
You are gone forever.

If we had only known,
Could we have saved you?
If we could have helped,
Would you have let us?
These are the questions,
We are doomed to ask for eternity.

We hope that you knew,
How much you meant to us.
You walked into our lives,
As if you had been there all along.
Then you disappeared.

But we will not forget,
In our hearts you live on,
As a brightly shining star,
Shining in our eyes.
Though you were led astray,
Our memories will hold you close…

Always

We love you and keep you with us forever.
Richard Henry Warren
1956-1999

Cry Love Give

I am Crying my Heart out Right here.
It is Sadness and Tragedy
and Overwhelming grief…
Perhaps my Heart won't Ever truly Return
until my Love has Entered again Evermore.
I would Give you A promise
To always Cherish and Hold true
and Everyday of Life to Love only you.

Colors

Every time I am away from you,
The colors in my life, all turn blue.
My sun fades away, yellow no more,
The dark green grass, turns to gray.
The flowers have no color,
The stars do not even shine.
When you are away, life is not as beautiful.
I await for your return,
To be in your arms,
And watch the world come alive,
Once more.

Fallen Stars

Audrey's shy beauty,
Anne and her laugh,
Heath, with that smile,
Gregory, his taps.

Jonathan, those eyes,
River's quiet pain,
Kurt and his voice,
Johnny's late night name.

Ronald the leader,
Anna so lost,
Pat's dear bravery,
For Brad, fame had a cost.

Christopher, tireless,
Suzanne's husky voice,
Brandon so promising,
Evel and his toys.

How the stars fall,
All gone too soon.
Inspiration to many,
You so brightened our moods.

Friendship...Love

Friendship...What a wonderful thing.
A person to lean on,
When your soul,
Cannot stand on its own.
A person to share,
Your laughter and memories.

Friendship...What if?
When those boundaries change,
What am I to do,
When instead of a shoulder to cry on,
I would rather have,
Your arms tight around me?

Friendship...What happens?
What if this friendship is no longer enough,
And I want to be more,
Than just your friend?
Because now,
I feel differently.

Friendship...Love.
If I tell you,
Will you stay there,
By my side?
Or will I lose you,
Completely?

Forgive, Not Forget

You knocked on my door,
In the middle of the night,
A smile on your face,
Your eyes shining bright.

"What do you want?"
I heard myself say.
You answered: "I think we should talk,
I have come a long way."

Calm was your voice,
I once so enjoyed,
This time, your assumptions,
Simply left me annoyed.

"Why after all this time?"
Was my questioning reply,
With you standing there,
As if we had never had our fight.

Could there be redemption for this man,
Who had hurt me so much?
Though I still get weak,
At the thought of his touch.

I do not know why,
Perhaps I will never be sure,
I moved aside slowly,
And let you walk through my door.

Maybe, because I am older,
You could still cause my heart harm,
But I want to ignore our past,
And feel only your arms.

I cannot forget,
I will try to forgive,
So I can be with you,
And in love I will live.

Feels Like Confusion

Whether I am in your arms
Or in your sight
The world seems to fill
With a brilliant light.
It has never felt like this before
Feels like confusion
Showed up at my door.
Why do I feel
So safe with you?
These feelings came so fast
I don't know what to do.
Do I let you get close
And risk a heartbreak?
Or do I spend time away
And let my heart ache?
Sometimes I wonder
What this is all for
Like how in the daylight
You hide from the world
Then when we're alone
And the whole world is asleep
You never miss the chance
To sweep me off my feet.
I can't ask you these questions
Or tell you how I feel
But I do know inside
These debates are so real.
Do I deny my own heart
And let my cold side win
Or do I break through the ice
And let your heart in?

Maybe I will just wait
Through the test of time
And hope in the end
Your heart will be mine.

Goodbye

You walked away,
And left me alone.
You did not know then,
I could stand on my own.

I do not need you,
Always hanging around,
Adding constant drama,
Dragging me down.

So many years it took
So very long,
For me to see,
I could finally be strong.

Off with you now.
Do not beg to return,
I have seen the light,
And from my mistakes, learned.

I need you no more,
Perhaps never did.
I have gained the new knowledge,
And, of you I am well rid.

I loved you once,
It was not wrong,
So much has been gained,
From your heartbreaking con.

Goodbye now, old love,

I must too walk away,
And start my new life,
Beginning today.

Each Day

My love for you,
Grows stronger each day.
No matter how close,
Or how far away.
Listening to,
Your soft, sweet voice,
I know in my soul,
I have made the right choice.
To be by your side,
Forever I will stay,
For the rest of my life,
Each hour, each day.

A Lullaby for My Son

(To be sung to the tune of Brahms' Lullaby)

In my arms,
Close your eyes.
Fall asleep my sweet angel.

Mama loves you,
Baby boy,
And will always hold you tight.

Sleep sound,
Sleep in peace,
Dream for awhile.

When you wake,
Little Love,
It will be with a smile.

Lessons Learned

You taught me so many things,
You taught me how to take a chance,
To dive in head first,
Into the deep sea of trust.
How to sleep peacefully,
Wrapped inside your arms.
You taught me how to love again,
And to reach for the stars.
Then, you taught me how to fall.
You forgot to tell me,
That you could not be trusted,
You could not be loved,
Or love anyone besides yourself.
I spoke to you a short time ago,
Tell me again,
How miserable you are,
Within the sorry existence,
Which you have created for yourself.
Of all you have taught me,
The best lesson,
Was the one I learned on my own.
I can fall gracefully,
Landing on my feet,
I can hold my head up high,
I can stand alone,
Peaceful and strong.

Safe Passage

As I watched her descend
From her palace in the trees
I was captivated by her beauty
And dropped to my knees.

"Do you seek wealth and glory?"
She asked me that day.
I replied "I seek only safe passage
As I go on my way."

"For there are dangers untold,
Hidden in this wood.
And I must overcome evil,
To triumph in good."

She looked down on my face
And saw there the truth,
For I could not hide from her,
My eyes held the proof.

She wrapped me in a cloak
And bade me to eat
Then sung me to sleep
In a voice more than sweet.

I awoke easily
Renewed and refreshed.
It was time to be on my way
But first to her make a pledge.

I would do what I must
To fulfill my quest
And when I had finished
Return to her for a rest.

I would tell her my tale
My lovely, dear queen
Who stepped into my path
As if from a dream.

As I set off again
With her army to protect me,
I saw her ascend once again
To her palace in the trees.

Those Arms

A friend once asked
Where is "favorite place to be"?
I used to reply
"In the arms of my love."
Those arms are still there,
But now the arms of a friend.
Both are wonderful to have around me,
But it is far more exciting
When they belong
To the one you would give everything for.
In my loneliness
I have created a better place,
That no one may ever shatter,
For it is built in the depths of my dreams
And decorated with my imagination.

My Sisters

Though we are separate people,
We share a history together,
That is like no other
In our lives.

With my good fortune,
Your eyes fill
With tears of happiness.
When troubled times befall me,
Your arms surround me
While my own tears
Stream down my face.

This eternal bond
Will never be broken.
You are always my best friend,
Even when at times,
We are bitter enemies.

You are my solid ground,
The pedestal I stand on, when I shine.
And I yours.

I love you
More than anyone else will understand,
But you do, as only you can,
Because you are my sisters!

Powerful Beauty

It flashes across the sky,
Reaches over the land,
Like delicate, deadly fingers,
Of a higher power's hand.

Its colors so bold,
So frightening and bright,
Like nature's fireworks,
That light up the night.

Its thunderous warning,
Follows close when it is near,
Though its beauty is great,
Its power we should fear.

Forget and Remember

In the blink of an eye,
So sudden, so soon,
I feel like I lost,
My sun and my moon.
I am left all alone,
Just to wonder why,
And all I can do to about it,
Is just sit here and cry.
The fire in my heart,
That warm and burning blaze,
Seems to have turned,
Into a cold and icy glaze.
My heart is now closed,
Never to re-open,
I cannot take a chance,
It will again get broken.
Someday I may forget,
How hard these eyes had cried,
But always will I remember,
The love that was deep inside.

One Day

One day I will be able
To tell my family
That I have truly lived my life.

I have few regrets,
For though I have made mistakes,
They have made me
Who I am today.

I have done crazy things,
And felt exhilaration as a reward.
Sometimes to conquer your fears,
You have to look them in the eyes.

I have been skydiving,
Flown through the clouds like a bird,
And with my parachute,
Drifted back to earth
Like a feather gliding in the breeze.

I have been parasailing.
Pulled by a boat,
And surfing the wind,
Like a kite, as if held by a child.

I have ridden the mechanical bull,
Holding on to the saddle,
Then falling to the floor.
But, for a moment,
I was a rodeo queen.

I have sung in public,
Letting my voice
Float from my body.

I have danced on stage,
Feeling my inner self
Releasing itself into the open,
As if being freed of its prison.

I have tattoos,
Making the fabled blue rose,
A reality on my skin.

I have become a mother,
Knowing for the first time,
What true happiness is,
And what I was meant to do, all my life.

And so, I say to you,
Live your life,
Take chances, make changes,
Be who you are...
Be free!
Then you can pass your life's tale
Onto your future generations.
One day...

An Evening at the Beach

I feel the warm, but quickly cooling sand beneath me,
The smell of salt, radiating from the sea fills my head.
The calming breeze blows all around me,
As it joins the sounds of the breaking waves,
To sing me the harmonious lullaby, so sweet to my ears.
The sun sets leaving a streak of light, across the dark waters,
Glowing like fire.
I am completely at peace as I absorb my surroundings.
I close my eyes.

I open them to find myself in reality.
The now cool sands are my soft sheets and pillow beneath my body.
The soothing wind, comes from the fan, blowing over my bed.
The blaze of the sleepy sun become the first rays of dawn,
Peeking into my bedroom.
My sweet song has turned into the demon alarming me awake,
To begin a new day.
Still longing for the peaceful solitude of my imagination,
I rise.

The Path Home

My head filled with riddles,
Oh what should I do?
I need to think clearly,
Can anyone help me?

I seem to have lost my way,
And know not where to turn.
I must fight for myself,
Where do I begin?
How will I know the right path?

I need to find light in the dark,
Before it is too late.
Begging, pleading, crying, hurting,
Are not my answers.

A warrior I must become,
And battle for the truth,
Only then can I find my way home.

For You...My Love

I never believed,
I could be so happy.
You inspire me,
To live and breathe,
Every moment of life,
To the fullest extent of my being.

You broke through the walls,
That I had surrounding,
My frightened heart.
Your soft touches,
And thoughtful actions,
Touch me so deeply.

I never wonder,
Where I stand.
I know I am always welcome,
By your side.
Your words so sweet,
And arms so safe,
I feel like I am dreaming.

There is but one more thing,
Left for me to say,
And I say it,
With strength and pride,
From very deep within my heart,
As I have never felt before:
I Love You.

The First Moments

From the moment I first knew
That you were growing inside me,
I felt surprise...

The very first time I heard
Your fast, little heartbeat,
I felt joy...

From the moment I first knew
Those flutters were your tiny feet,
I felt wonder...

The very first time I saw
You moving around inside my womb,
I felt blessed...

From the moment I saw
Your sweet face and held you in my arms,
I knew love...

Friendship

Life is full of friends
That come and go.
Battles and arguments
High and low.
Different friends
Different times
Through these battles
Peace will chime.
Up in the years
The road will bend
The truest friends
Will be there at the end.

Who Knew?

Who knew you could find,
Such happiness in a smile?
A kiss brightens my whole day,
Your sweet hugs are my nourishment.

Who knew someone so small,
Could mean so much?
You give my life meaning.
Now that I have you,
I would be nothing with you.

Who knew the most important thing I would ever do,
Would be to raise you?
My child, my dreams, my very reason for being,
You have blessed my life in so many ways,
Without ever knowing.

Who knew you could love someone so much?
My darling son, my angel,
I cherish every moment with you,
And gaze upon you with wonder,
And unconditional love.

My Stars and Sky

You look through me,
As if I were glass,
Into my heart and soul
And into my past.
Your safe warm arms,
Are always there.
With you the world could fall
And I would hardly care.
You are my moon and sun,
My stars and sky,
I feel my heart melt,
When I look into your eyes.
Falling in love with you
Will be the greatest adventure.
Being in your arms,
I could do forever.

Stay

You asked me to take you with me,
I quietly answered "no".
I saw the painful look in your eyes,
When I said you could not go.

I thought I needed to stand alone,
For once in my life.
If only I could have known,
You would never again be by my side.

I was trying to play it safe,
I tried to play it smart.
Instead of listening to my head,
I should have answered my own heart.

What I would not give,
To go back to that sad day,
And change the course of time,
By asking you to stay.

I would gladly take your hand,
And hold you in my arms.
I could gaze into those crystal, blue eyes,
That made me feel so safe and warm.

Forgive me love, for I am lost,
And what I say now is true,
I am no longer afraid of being in love,
Just of a lifetime without you.

Most of All

Dry your eyes, my only love,
For I was sent from Heaven above.
To guide you, your whole life through,
And to take special care of you.
I am your angel, we heard your prayers,
And I do promise to always be here.
I will come when you call,
Catch you when you fall,
And love you forever,
Most of all.

Remember

I remember that day,
So very well,
I watched through my tears,
As each tower fell.

The smoke and dust,
And dirt and debris,
Made a clouded blanket
Over the city.

Now and again
My broken heart would serge,
As rarely but sometimes
A saved life would emerge.

Another report
More lives would be gone
As another taken plane,
Crashed our dear pentagon.

My breath in my chest
Caught with a hitch
At the sight of yet another
Downed plane in a ditch.

Our horror at knowing
Our old world had changed
As someone had hurt us
For personal gain.

Realization had come,
Our lives torn apart,
We were now at war,
New York was the heart.

We must always remember,
Those taken that day,
All our lives it changed,
That tragic September, on the eleventh day.

The Key

An impossible feat,
I have heard it said,
Never to be conquered.
I call it, "my wall,"
For I am the designer.
To climb it would be to find,
That it ends at the gates of Heaven.
To tunnel below,
To the depths of Hell.
To break it down,
Would shatter the tools,
As well as the man.
To go around it,
Is to find that it ends,
Where it began.
There is but one way in,
Through a well hidden door,
Invisible to the ordinary eye.
This door is heavily locked and guarded,
And only one holds the key,
Though he does not yet know,
That it is in his possession.
This is the key to my heart,
Through "my wall,"
Which I have built around it.

Summer Kisses

We were there in the dark
One summer night,
Laughing, and talking,
Flirting alike.

I remember thinking
How nice, how fun,
As we lingered discussing
Everything under the sun.

We lay side by side,
On the bedroom floor,
Singing November Rain,
Then laughing some more.

You pulled me close
Your lips found mine,
Such comfort I felt,
That one evening in time.

The following year,
It happened again,
One lovely kiss,
And then returned to
Just friends.

All these years later
I still remember the touch
Of those sweet summer kisses
I have cherished so much.

More Than You Know

I Love You,
More than you could possibly know.
As each day goes by,
My love for you continues to grow.
I hope you will always be here,
By my side,
Through all the tears and happiness.
Every time our lips touch,
I am mesmerized by thoughts,
Of nothing but pure love for you.
When I see your eyes,
Looking into mine,
I know our love is meant to be.

Q & A

"Wise men say, only fools rush in."?
(Elvis Presley)
Brave women say, "Hold on tight, here we go!"

"Burn the midnight oil"?
Relax and enjoy your night in your own way,
You worked hard enough all day.

"All that we see or seem, is but a dream
Within a dream"?
(Edgar Allan Poe)
Dreams are nice, but reality is truth.

"That's the power of love"?
(Huey Lewis and the News)
No, it's probably just lust,
And probably great quantities of alcohol.

"Sow your wild oats"?
As long as you remember where they were planted.
Too wild, can be disastrous.

"Listen to your heart"?
(Roxette)
No! Listen to your head,
So you don't end up on the couch with a box of tissues,
Eating ice cream from the container.

"Just say no"?
Sometimes it is more fun to scream "Yes!"

"The glass is half full"?
And, that's a problem? Hell, drink it!

"The glass is half empty"?
Refill it and move on,
It's not rocket science.

"What becomes of a broken heart"?
(Westlife)
It repairs itself just in time
For the next loser to break it.
Ah, the endless circle of love.

"Oh say can you see,
By the dawn's early light"?
(Francis Scott Key)
How about noon's early light?
Then I'll see whatever you want.

"Life is not measured by
The amount of breaths we take,
But by the moments,
That take our breath away"?
Okay, explain drowning then.
Seriously, romance me all you want,
But I do need to breathe.

"Working like a dog"?
(The Beatles)
When was the last time your dog did anything,
Besides lay in the sunlight all day,
Unless you offer it food.

"All I have to do is dream"?
(The Everly Brothers)
Wake up before life passes you by completely!

"Words to live by"?
Whatever!
Actions speak louder than words!

Growth and Warmth

I watch the breeze,
So cool under the warm sun,
Blowing them softly,
As they grip for life,
With their tiny, brown fingers.
Their silky hair sways,
All around the little, pink faces,
As they look towards the light,
For growth and warmth.
Surrounded by others they sit,
In the sun and breeze,
Waiting to become full and strong.

Specters of Adulthood

As a child, I was a believer in ghosts.
At times, adorable creatures,
Seeking only friendship.
Most often were the frightening, bodiless beings,
Attempting to steal from the living,
What they had themselves lost.

The spirits of my youth are no longer.
As a woman, I know the truth.

The specters which haunt our adulthood,
Are only shadows of our past.
They linger beside us,
Reminding us always, of who we once were.
They are the walls of the homes
Where we now reside.
The stepping stones which pave the road ahead,
Leading us to who we are to become.

We need not fear our ghosts,
Only embrace the lessons they would teach.
Understand that we are never truly free from ourselves,
As we are our own,
Lifelong companions.

Spark

The strangest feeling has come over me,
It seems my whole life there has been
This little spark inside me, waiting to ignite.
When I met you, that spark burst into life,
And lit my whole world ablaze.
There is a fire in my heart, that makes me feel,
Alive and awake for the first time.
I can trust and feel like never before.
In your arms, is the safest place I have ever been.
Your kiss melts my heart,
And makes my head feel dizzy.
Your touch sends shivers through my body and soul.
When you are away from me,
My heart aches until your return.
You have shown me a strength and weakness,
About myself that I never knew existed.
Never before have I felt so comfortable,
In so short a time.
So, for all of these wonderful things,
I thank you,
But, most of all,
For just being you.

My Beautiful Children

Cora Lyn

Candid, yet considerate
Observant more than given credit
Rare beauty in one so young
Ablaze with charisma

Lovely and patient
Youth lived to the fullest
Never forget how much I love you!

Tristan Cary

Trusting always
Ready to play all day long
I love you so much
Sweet and gentle
Tender and kind
A tornado of joy
Newcomer to our world

Cuddly and cute
A funny boy
Really makes me laugh
You are the light of my life!

Remembering My Angel

It has been many years,
Since that fateful night.
I lost my faith,
When you lost your life.
How could I ever forget,
That sweet smile, those dark eyes?
Time was not on our side.
I grew up.
You watched from above.
I think of you often,
Still with sadness,
That our memories are not more.
I hope that you found peace,
In your place of rest.
Happiness on Earth,
Was beyond your reach.
Maybe someday you will be waiting,
To take my hand,
And show me the way,
As I did with you,
The day we met.
This time we can be friends,
Instead of adult to child,
Walking hand in hand through eternity.
I want you to know,
You will always be my Angel,
Even then, because

That is how you have remained,
In my memory for so long.
I hope that you know,
I will always continue to remember.

(In Memory of Danny Rodriquez
1988-1994)

Silence in Darkness

I am bound to him,
By the ring on my hand,
My tormentor,
In the guise of husband.

My dearest knight,
Showers me in kindness
His love he shows,
By waiting in silence.

Trapped in this castle,
The monster standing guard,
While I dream of a world
Wrapped in my love's arms.

Each night in my sleep,
High walls the demon cannot penetrate
Deep in my dreams,
For him I do not have to wait.

I kiss his lips
So soft and so sweet
Lay my head on his chest
Listening to his heartbeat.

As morning arrives,
The blue skies return,
Leaving my loves arms
I feel the sun burn.

One day I will,
I promise, be released
Of this evil of man,
My nightmare ceased.

In your arms,
I will stay, so safe and so warm.
Happy we will be
For our evermore!

Waiting

Without you,
I feel so alone,
Always waiting,
For you to come home.
Waiting to feel,
Your arms around me,
Looking into your eyes,
As clear and cool,
As the deep, calm sea.
I will be walking on air,
As they say,
When finally
You are home to stay.
So happy forever,
I will be with you,
When there is no more,
Waiting to do.

Questions of Love

Why is it...
The ones who love the most
Lose love so quickly?

Have you ever...
Laid in someone's arms
Wishing, hoping, dreaming
You could be there forever?

How come...
In the blink of an eye,
Everything is gone?

Like night into day,
Wishing hoping dreaming
Becoming cold lonely reality.

Is it possible...
To find a safe, warm place
Where there is no line
Between fantasy and reality?

Where is...
The one who wishes for me,
For my arms around him,
My lips to kiss, and skin to touch?

When will I...
Finally be able to love,
Without the heartbreak
That always follows?

Do I...
Forever have to be guilty
Of opening my heart and soul,
Only to have it shattered?

Can there be...
A person who fits
My heart and soul
As if they have always been there,
And without each other
We could not exist?

Are there...
Any answers to the questions I ask?
Or will it always be more riddles of life
Instead of eternal happiness?

I know...
I have found who I believe,
To be the one for me.

Asleep and awake,
Night and day,
I spend wishing, hoping, dreaming,
That one day he will,
Find me as well.

Will he...
Be here to stay?
Or will he walk away,
Leaving once more
The circle of questions to take his place,
Waiting to be answered?

My heart and soul
Again trying to repair the pain,
Wishing, hoping, dreaming
For some release
From the hard, cold wall,
I have built to keep them hidden away.

Spring

The sun shines down,
So warm, so bright.
It wakes the world,
From its cold, gray slumber.
The air all around me,
Brings heat to my body,
While the cool breeze,
Fills my lings,
With fresh, crisp air.
Spring has begun,
Plant life is all abloom.
Finally we rid ourselves,
Of our wintry burden.

You Brought Me to Life

We knew this had to end,
Right from the start.
I know walking away from you,
Will break my poor heart.

We knew the risk,
What was at stake.
For the first time in years,
I have a heart to ache.

Wrapped in your arms,
Warm against you in bed,
You brought me to life,
Resurrected me from the dead.

You were never supposed to happen,
We were completely unexpected,
Yet here I am,
My soul so affected.

You showed me I could walk,
Back into the world,
My head held high,
My hand in yours, curled.

Soon comes the day,
I know we both fear,
When from your life,
I must disappear.

You returned my life,
Now I send you towards yours.
This is not the place for you,
You deserve so much more.

Take some chances,
Be confident, be true.
And know in my heart,
I will always love you!

Spirits of My Youth *is a collection of poems,*
"based" on life experiences.
Whatever emotion you are seeking,
you will find within these pages.
Carissa Lynn Taylor captures the human heart
And sets it aflame!

A native of Haverhill, Massachusetts, Carissa Lynn Taylor now resides in Lake Saint Louis, Missouri with her young son. She is a full-time mother, and part-time student of Anthropology. She dreams of one-day taking her family to see Egypt.
This is Carissa's first published works.